Unbeknownst

Unbeknownst

Julie Hanson

University of Iowa Press ≈ Iowa City

University of Iowa Press, Iowa City 52242
Copyright © 2011 by Julie Hanson
www.uiowapress.org
Printed in the United States of America

Design by Sara T. Sauers

The University of Iowa Press is a member of Green Press
Initiative and is committed to preserving natural resources.

Printed on acid-free paper

ISBN-13: 978-1-58729-964-3
ISBN-10: 1-58729-964-X
LCCN: 2010936668

for J. M. S.

Contents

III ≈

Acknowledgments

GRATEFUL THANKS TO the editors of the following journals where these poems, or versions of them, first appeared: "Praemeditatio," *32 Poems Magazine*; "Long Dance, Slow Revolution," *Ascent*; "Remedial Weeding," the *Cincinnati Review*; "Hurdle," *Columbia: A Magazine of Poetry & Prose*; "Covenant," *Crab Orchard Review*; "Flow," *Daily Palette*; "Instead," *Fulcrum*; "Scant," the *Iowa Review*; "Only Hat" and "Always a Little Something Somewhere in the Purse," *New Ohio Review*; "Larger," *Poetry East*; "Boy at Dusk," RUNES: *A Review of Poetry*; "Under November," the *Saint Ann's Review*; "Table for Three" and "The Anxiety of the Pilgrim," *Tampa Review*; "Allocation," *Terrain.org: A Journal of the Built & Natural Environments*. "Remedial Weeding" appeared also on *Poetry Daily*.

For timely recognition and generous gifts I am indebted to the National Endowment for the Arts, the Vermont Studio Center, Timothy Murphy, and the Directors of the West Chester University Conference on Narrative and Form.

I'm indebted to the several generations of my Iowa City writing group for serious consideration of poems and drafts long preceding these; for their own good examples of what can be done; for the meetings themselves, in providing an excellent and compelling reason to generate work; and to the current and long-standing members, especially, for their measured judgment and ready counsel: Kathy Hall, Dan Lechay, Jim McKean, and Jan Weissmiller.

I'm grateful to the congregation and ministers of Peoples Church Unitarian Universalist of Cedar Rapids, Iowa, 1987–present, who have provided constant occasion for meaningful engagement with the world, countless opportunities to be of use, and plenty of good reasons to do so.

I am grateful for Richard Hanson and for Will Hanson, who have steadied and sustained me, who have inspired me, and laughed.

I ≈

Use the Book

I love this book, I was telling someone
the other day; it's as if the pages have been
rinsed with tea and dried in the sun, gentle
on the eye and wanting your touch. Old jacket,
favorite hat, pages so soft they whisper right on by.
Perfect for fishing, although the poems
have little or nothing to do with Nature.
Looking up from those surreal and strictly human
situations into all this, then, is such a surprise:
I thought I saw a muskrat there, just the other side
of the stream, standing near that clump
of darker grass . . . oh he's slipped into the water,
he's gone now, you've missed him completely.
Wait, see the head? He's making straight for our
stringer! Pull it up, pull it up! Well then, at least
hit him on the head with something. Take this.

Double Bed

My eyes anchored on a word in the book
and the thought-waters of the day
flooded over it, mucked-up,
disobedient, and then (the knot
must have slipped—for how many moments
did I drift?) a small bump of arrival
and I read another sentence, no more,
before an incoming phrase pulled me
someplace else, indifferent to the text.
Enough was enough. I closed the book.
I threw the extra pillow over there,
put the book aside and sank.
I sprawled: *the whole bed to myself.*

The room below me launched into my head,
the cluttered surfaces of the floor
and of my desk, the scattered pencils,
ashtray, matches, cigarettes,
the fan of papers, short stacks of books.
Then the image trembled slightly, no more
than a rabbit's caution in the grass.
There was import here, and that came next
in a close-up on the ashtray with its last
cigarette. *Yes, I'm sure,* I thought,
to extinguish the idea, implausible
and plainly paranoid, only come to me
in opportunity, since was I not,
for now, the sole parent home?

Still, it was not the kind of thought
I often had. *Go down and check.*
I fell asleep imagining the smoldering
that would begin in the papers,
their corners turning gray, scrolling
one onto the other, sending down
a fragile threadline of orange, the supply
of oxygen diminishing, the smoke
unnoticed in the density of sleep,
and then my desk become the perfect fuel
for that initial push of flames
until the fire beneath us was full-fledged,
and when I awoke what was burning
was the sun, full up and brilliant.

Betrayal (A Valentine)

Sometimes I tell my husband things completely without thinking
as if the items in my day were dishes rinsed and slipped into the washer after lunch
and forgotten for all the afternoon as they cycle through sani-wash and rinse and dry,
ending with that little click that lets us know they're done, and then as we stand
in the kitchen slicing vegetables for salad and getting out the butter for the bread,
I remember the dishes that are surely done and one by one I take them out
with no concern about their likely interest as artifacts to anyone
and that is how I came to mention that Jean had told me something, a secret
that wasn't deeply personal, just something she didn't want let out
until afterwards, if, in fact, she got the job at all. But don't mention it to anyone,
I said, remembering that she had said she hadn't told anyone about it yet,
and now, thanks to me and unbeknownst to her, she had.
On the very next night we gave Jean a ride to a church event and before she even had
her seat belt fastened, my husband introduced the topic of the job she was trying for
which he wasn't supposed to know anything about and spoke for the entire ride
and without pause about matters he was privileged to know concerning it.
I was driving, yes, but I didn't feel to be the one in control.
Well, I could have killed him.
Technically, it was myself who had done wrong and yet as this was happening
I felt that it was me whom someone had betrayed, because I really do not want
the kind of marriage where one person hesitates before mentioning a thing
(thinking, oops, oh wait now, do I need to censor that from him?); I'd rather have
the kind of marriage where nothing is pre-sorted or arranged for presentation,
where the plates, be they china or the everyday, are set out without pretense or apology,
and where each companion knows with an automatic generosity
what to do with what is shared. On the other hand, how I do admire that Jean
expects this kind of sensitivity from friends.

Flow

I like the bare feet, the cotton knit crop pants and simple sleeveless tee,
I like unrolling the mat with a snap of the wrists, whipping it out on the floor
like a frog hurling out its tongue down on the pond in the mist.
I like the dimmed down lighting of the room.
I like the balancing poses like tree and eagle and warrior three
and being reminded of where we fold in half,
the symmetry of every action taken
being taken once again on the other side. And the ujjayi breathing
which enters and exits only through the nose, but does so
audibly, the wave of breath rolling out until all that's left is the last
uneven edge of it and then how it has to come back.
I like the way I don't think once about civil litigation
until long after we've come out of corpse pose and said namaste.
I like thinking of my hip as a melting block of ice
as I slip deeper into pigeon. I like all these animal names,
and the stretch in the back of the legs, and the twists
and the nearly indistinguishable versions of the sun salutation,
and the bridge, the plow, and the face of the cow. I like the mild complaints
from the rear of the room, the pleadings for an extra long savasana
at the end of the hour. I like feeling that my torso has actually lengthened
when I've been reminded once again to lengthen it.
I like rolling up my mat and exiting through the revolving door,
surprised by a blast of heat or by the rain, and by the perfect fit
of my shoes and the ease of my gait, and how I slip in and fold
behind the wheel into the driver's seat like a thin young thing:
My organs are surely glistening. This car was made for me.

His Dream

I rolled over and looked at my husband.
"I just had your dream," I said. "What?"
he said. "Isn't that impossible?"
"You'd think so," I said. "I can't see why
that dream should come to me. You're
the one with the job, the one with the colleagues and bosses."
I said this because these were the people
who'd peopled the dream. It was Christmas,
time for the year-end event, and, although
in reality we'd decided not
to attend, in the dream I'd put on
that same black dress and prepared to feel
as I always did when it came time
to stroll among the tables set for ten:
that wherever we would sit
would turn out to be unfortunate.
I was therefore surprised to find
that each couple had instead
a small table to themselves!
Still, the atmosphere was hardly
intimate. And the dream didn't
indicate where single people sat
or were supposed to sit.
But for Charles, the father, and for Charles,
his son, and their wives, two tables
had been spread with Irish linen.
Thick white napkins draped their laps
and dangled to their shins.

Their wine was sultry and slow
and practically black, the leaded
crystal goblets instantly refilled.
Their silver was heavy and the forks
had a nice long head.
My husband and I cut up our stroganoff
with stainless forks and knives
and drank a recent vintage from Crate
& Barrel glasses. Our tablecloth
was gingham. Our napkins were red.
I almost didn't notice poor Arlene,
still waiting with her husband
in their corner booth—it was so dark
with all that knotty paneling.
Their table was linoleum with metal trim.
The water for their glasses was as yet
unpoured. They tugged their napkins from
a chrome dispenser on the table top
and flattened them as best they could
across their laps, but the napkins were,
alas, destined for the floor.
Then I noticed Tom, gliding
Joan across the room—I could hear the word
"enchanting" as they neared—and Joan
 exclaiming softly, (yet we could hear
 her every word) "and such attention
 has been given to every single detail
 of this evening!" They stood, glowing pinker,

beneath the central chandelier,
while all that was around them
began to slowly spin—the muraled walls,
the potted palms, and all the tables, even theirs,
its menus overturned. "That's incredible!"
my husband said, and sat straight up
in bed, "although I thought the focus
was sustained a bit too long
on the paper napkins, didn't you?,
and the dream never did provide
any flatware for Arlene and Don."
"You're right, you're right," I said.
"Mismatched sets, or plastic?"
"Plastic by all means," he said, "but let's
give their booth a window. Let's put them
on a train." "Can't manage that," I said,
"The dream is done. It's not like
it's a poem. I'm not going to spend
the next ten years revising it.
And, anyway, a vacation trip
for Arlene and Don is clearly not in keeping
with the correspondences ordained."
"You know," my husband said,
"for someone who often claims
to stand outside of this—sometimes
bewildered, sometimes alarmed—
your every contribution to this dream
seems awfully well-informed."

Instead

My brother called from Madison while I was out and left a message
of thirty bitter words, and he intends to tell our father
out in Tucson not to speak with me again by phone.
Apparently it has not occurred to him that in scenes
he never glimpsed there may have been some need for patience
and for arbitration which his sensitivities have altogether failed to guess.
The limits of his imagination are too lengthy to list!

A family of three or four is too complex!

We think we see the possibilities and forget we have imagined them.
Each small gesture to accommodate is another chance
to flub it up and take a walk instead. Then I spied the one
streetlight near our home running at quarter power,
barely glowing, almost out. As I pointed and related this
to my companion, it came on strong. How telling, I thought,
and so like an object to offer a guiltless and forthright response.

Promise

People do not like
to be reminded of
promises they have made.

It puts them in the
adult mode, having
to disappoint a child
with a truer reality.
That was then, this is
now. I will drop off
the dry cleaning. I will
be at the meeting on
Thursday. I will pick up
the children after school.
I will bring it next time.
I'll remember. I will
always love you. I will
never leave you.

Notice how with the
promise there is so much
in front of it. It can also
represent a false report
about something that has
allegedly transpired. Your
name is down for
that. I took care of it.
He never mentioned

that, I assure you.
Believe me. Honest.
I would never kid you
on this. Absolutely.
Perish the thought.

Notice the use of wide
words, taking so much
in. And how hard it is
to read them, or hear them
—say, on the telephone—
without at the same
time seeing the hands,
the presentation of
the countenance and head,
familiar as you are
with exactly how they must
be poised,
exactly where
they're going next.

Scant

I planted those seeds bitterly. What good could
come of them? Though the moon was new,
though the rain began before I was done,
I scattered them hurriedly and without real hope.

For hadn't last year's winter garden been well in
by then? A good two weeks earlier, yet nothing much
had flourished—a few small leaves from the hardiest
seeds. The very minimum, apparently.

II≈

Criterion for Sleep

Disarmament, and dark, like the pond is dark
when it's in bloom, dark like the bark of sugar
maples seen between leaves which have been
caught between yellow and red in such a way
that there's a suggestion, too, of pink. Beauty
then, is it? Or simplicity: the pine floor,
pine chair, blue bowl, and the sound of a cricket.
Welcome routines. And not a dear thing
has been wasted. Nothing left over
in the machine of the brain to be tumbled and banked,
the fit is snug and the rag rug is satisfied
with the warmth of the cat. The only ceremony
is to breathe without hearing the breath, to leave here
temporarily. Enough is enough.

Balance

Whatever I prepare, my brother will not eat.
Any letter I write to him, my brother will not read.
I can say now that we've been like gods, our powers
wasted. Whatever he tells me collapses in my trust.
Whatever he speaks of is harder to love.
No one remembers the first injustice.
Gone are its properties as food. And yet,
I have brightened inside, having seen sign
of his happiness. How lucky he looked then!
How surprised that such a thing could befall him.
"Sign of," I say, since I wasn't one to know its source.
Sometimes I thought that I'd rather not know,
but that was the real me thinking.

Table for Three

We made our selections without much deliberation.
We all went for the same.

Our waiter returned with the tea. The tea was
—we'd never had a tea like it before.

I said it was somber. It seemed familiar . . .
Roasted corn, our waiter told us,

and after that it tasted more like broth to me,
but it was the perfect complement

to everything. The spicy cold cabbage,
the sushi and tempura, the rice and teriyaki.

We were subdued as we ate. It was very unlike us.

We'd asked our questions on the drive there
and our son had answered them.

Seated at Aoeshe, we had little left to say.

My attention was drawn now and then
to my neck and face, my forearms and wrists,

I think because of the circulating air. It felt good
to be reminded of the skin that way,

with no discomfort whatsoever, only pleasure.
Just beyond the stainless steel,

the one chef visible to us was preparing
sushi, we supposed, or shaving carrots

into butterflies that would come to rest
atop the dab of wasabi on each plate.

His gestures were snake-quick
and lost to us, but accurate, reminding us

to notice the presentation of the food before us,
even to the spacing of the shapes.

We lifted bowls between our hands and drank.
We turned our hands into cranes and fed ourselves with beaks.

Remedial Weeding

You don't need to know its name
to know it is a weed; if it
has taken hold between two
paving bricks, if its thin root
or complex undermop is wedged
where the concrete riser joins the concrete step,
then assuredly it is.
It is redundant, stubborn work,
to which you squat or kneel or bend,
moving lowly in one manner
or another over the entire area
to be covered so that, naturally,
afterwards, you'll ache.

And yet, what better use
could you have put these to:
one yellow-handled tool
and two tightening circles of thought?
For those times when the heart, still
resonant and stunned,
is dominant,
this is the kind of work you want,
where it is best to look
no more than one weed ahead,
and where the iron inability to set a course
drills the focus downwards
with single-mindedness and depth.

Hurdle

They use this argument
against the most obstinate:
a stick, and a portable wall
shoved in its face
when it tries to veer off.
Pig, pig, what can it
be thinking of?
Is it aware that the man
walks by its side, ready,
with a square yard of flat
hard space, to sever
the pig from where it would go?
Or do pig eyes see
so low and straight ahead
that, to the pig, the man
is completely out of
the picture? Not a force,
not a visitor?
And that's just life, after all:
wall, want, wall, want, wall?

Under November

I don't know why I woke up
so early. I found the door step
empty and the cold coming in.
It was too soon for the paper,
too dark for conversation.
I ate breakfast without reading.
Even when it came, more than
two hours later, daylight
had hardly any dawning.
The light bulbs in their sockets
worked, but they seemed past
their greatest power. I felt contained
in a tiny tale, the end of which
could almost be sensed. I thought
if I could just speak of this condition,
it might yet open to a different
one, ending with some stairs.
"It's so dark now," I said again
and again in the days to come,
sometimes aloud and to him,
as if the correct enunciation
of this short string of words
could brighten the interior.
If not for me, then for him.
I can't say why these were the words
I always found, nor what
he might have found to meet them with
but the simple "yes," a mirror

that wasn't angled properly.
After that he looked perplexed.
And the words never seemed to
help me to my meaning, but swept
the top of what that was,
speaking only of the season.

Always a Little Something Somewhere in the Purse

She was tall and blonde, although seated and plain.
I couldn't determine her age. She was trying not to look me in the face.
I was approaching a bank of blue seating at Gate B-8,
her bank of seating, and I sat next to her.
I got out my glasses and reading.
I put them back in my bag.
How could I read when the woman seated next to me and trying not to cry
was only mostly succeeding?
I rustled through the inner pockets of my purse
until I found the travel packet of tissue, crumpled from the years,
flecked with leather dust. But as I offered it up, I saw that she, *Thanks, anyway,*
had already produced her own.
Isn't that just like us?—always a little something somewhere in the purse
which can't alter reality in the large sense
but might help us along in the small.

Her phone rang.

She wiped her nose and answered with her name.
No, she couldn't show the split foyer this afternoon,
but Cindy in the office could.
Some kind of confidence had happened in her shoulders. And her voice:
genuine, helpful. She specified the freeways to avoid and better ways to take.
It sounded like L.A.
Her voice played the notes of continual possibility.
There was one more door at the end of disappointment,
and this might be it, it just might. Hearing her speak,
there isn't a client who wouldn't have straightened a bit,

curiosity increased.

She slipped her phone into her bag and rearranged her legs.

I glanced obliquely to our right and said,

"You handled that awfully well, Karen, under the circumstances."

Then she told me everything.

O'Hare International Airport

Allocation

Good night—you Princes of Maine,
you Kings of New England!
—John Irving, *The Cider House Rules*

Truth is, I entered my family rather straightforwardly.
I was a dime on a sidewalk, gleaming.

Whatever disorientation was borne
from the drop and the spin, the pocketing dark
and resettlement,
is reapportioned with benign intent
when I think of what awaits the clones
as they are told the stories of their origins.

Or, sooner to unfold and no easier,
the stories for those selves
who, through the planned accidents of their lives,
will lay down the precedents
for the reproductive future:

XX, who came from the hundredth
egg of a fetus never born.
Harvest of harvest. Daughter of none.

And XY, whose comatose father
was hardly involved.
So that to locate the male initiative
we really must visit his parents
whose grief, double-taxed and thereby emboldened,
jumped over the tomb.

Alms from the young.
Alms from the deeply unconscious.

Shall we call him Ditto whose very
mention brings all we meant instantly to mind?
Or shall we call him Xerox,
little word disjointed from its etymology,
little word that's hopped out, dry?

And if we call her Fay, coming to us from Faith,
who will stop her, when she's of an age,
from spelling it Fey,
which changes our meaning completely.
Winged instant of spirit, creature unreal.

Captured Possibilities, that's what you
even in your serums are, compilations of
the spoken for and the anonymous.

What neon colors will show up
in the regions of your fantasies,
what elements of randomness to spackle your dreams?
Who would dare project trajectories
for your identities? Who can think of you

and not, with their next thought,
begin? Those dewy blue eyes!
That cherubim skin! Those plump
dimpled knees and dear rumpled ears,
those opposable thumbs.

Someone waits for you, counting the days
to completion. Someone counts you
foremost among fortunes.
Yet surely will your days
step one by one before you,
and simply close behind you, done.

May your inventions all begin in paradox.
May your marketing be genuine.

Basis

Things were simpler then,
the early 1950s,
and things which seemed too sad

or difficult to say
sometimes went unmentioned.
Even formal documents

like these in which we think to find
absolute congruency
journeyed from the truth.

The trouble is, the ways around
a thing unsaid are myriad
and free, whereas chronology

isn't, not usually.
                    And so
these the records of my life
begin with a skip and a stutter,

the claims and authenticity of one
emptied by the dates
given deadpan by the other.

On page two, for instance,
where legally I'm born to them,
my age of eighteen months

has been inserted. Then my name
is granted to me, new,
which means in all the text

that's come before this
I'm the one I've never heard of.
Nothing can be fixed

about the circularity of this,
but in the space of these
few pages, a great deal

is amended which,
in the certificate of birth,
can be consolidated:

a woman lies down
in simple substitution
and does as she's told,

a different man discreetly
leaves and is awakened
with good news.

There is my birth-date,
a weight dropped into it
at ten p.m.
                    Only names

have been changed, a legality.
I think we are embarrassed
for these documents,

for their methods and their awkwardness,
for the problems that they meant
to fix, for the way they must,

of necessity, conflict.
And I am too cheaply thrilled
by mention of my prior name,

kept secret for so long,
maybe it's private.
                    What
is one to do with such a thing

even as it makes long-
settled things ring wrong
or right? Say, for instance,

it's the name you gave to a dog,
or the name of a town you came to stay in,
say that it's a name you've hated

ever since a certain incident
with a certain stupid dress,
say that it's a name

that seems to call you,
unaccountably, on every hard
or hidden thing you've done,

what then?
                    This name
is neither something meant to be
nor something never meant.

What can it represent?
I slept and dreamt,
I gazed and must have fed.

Alias from an alien life,
skipping stone of kryptonite,
remaindered tag from my creator,

treasure, relic, this is what:
you are too late to be a basis
and must stay astonishing.

Grab the Far End

Enough has been said.
We were certain it would.
No one could help me.
I did it myself.
I can't really blame them.
Consider the cost.
Remember the time.
A good chance of rain.
There goes the timer.
I feel like fish.
I don't have the time.
Remember the bomb.
The spring is broken.
I meant to tell you.
It doesn't matter.
The cut is infected.
There's simply no telling.
I really can't say.
Replace all the bearings.
Plug the meter.
I remember it well.
I allow that it does.
I imagine you do.
I never learned how.
That's a demerit!
To tell you the truth.
Just let it lie.
Stay out of the weeds.
It didn't come through.

We have some momentum.
I don't want to play.
Don't mind what I said.
Don't listen to me.
Pick up your jacket.
Measure it twice.
No wonder they moved.
This fudge is amazing.
I said that I had.
Imagine the outcome.
Forget about that.
Dredge it like this.
Not if I try.
I wish you would quit that.
Grab the far end.
I need more leverage.
The nail is rusty.
The railing is bent.
The water is fine.
Not that I know of.
Nobody wants it.
Anyone could.
The dog is barking.
The narrows are ripped.
Suspend your belief.
Right after he left her.
I was never so bored.
I dreaded the rest.
I'll never remember.

Untitled

Whiter by far than an egg
is the paper I haven't the wherewithal to fill,
its unblemished surface a reproach.

A good opportunity, it speaks of potential.

It's an assignment I don't understand.

It implicates my life with emptiness.
"Once," it says, "things happened,
and you were changed by them."

Larger

The female cardinal isn't the least bit
disappointed that the shade of red she is is brown.
She looks at him and thinks, Aren't we gorgeous?

Disappointment is a theme too available to me.
Judgment, another.
Would that I were rid of them.

I always turn to look too late into the leaves.
Of course there is the one remedy.
Wait.

Approval

Applause, then pats on the back, then personal notes,
and the referent event journeys on, less large
and less close. Tiny and comic, it waddles
to the top of the road. Finite and bright,
it has marked me and changed me, an ember
held in my palm a counted-out minute,
then blown. Mention, I think, reddens it.
Let's not encourage it. Remember
instead the acrobat who could not
remedy his cough. It was his far
awkwardness that engaged us. Really, his loops
were too close to the bar and unrelaxed
so that we had to watch his every move
and all the while a rival impulse
plunged us to the pavement
where we thought he might drop.
He thought he might drop right in that star,
we thought, and it must have been all he could do
to carry through, he couldn't have given
our approval a thought. Only at the very
last, when he stepped onto the disk
and turned, could he afford and could we risk
applause. Then, from that brief balcony,
he could request it: torso of accomplishment
in beams of crossing color, O marvel-
man, standing but a few slow
footfalls from the man he was: transitional,
forgetful, for the moment, that he needed us.

Only Hat

My sadness has the texture of a dime store balloon;
when I slide my hand across it, I get no pleasure from it.

My sadness has no merit whatsoever.

My sadness is a pose I cannot hold a moment longer, but I must
because I am in yoga class where this pose in particular would be
impossible to do had I understood it in advance,
yet when fed instructions bit by bit while bending back . . .
I can believe I just might get the hands.

My sadness stems from a bottomless blame. It knows
that it doesn't matter, does it, if the reason is legitimate.

My sadness is lonelier the longer I sit with it.

My sadness comes back to me; it is all my own.

My sadness has three corners, three corners has my hat.
I have chosen this, my sadness, over all available hats.
Firemen hats and nurses' hats, telephone line
repairmen hats. Military, ski, and Napoleon's only hat.

Difficult Fortunes

Wisdom
more quickly come
than it would have otherwise.

≈

Empty cookie.

≈

Yours is favorable,
mine is a duplicate.

≈

An admonishment too late to be
interpreted as warning.

Boy at Dusk

What are you doing, chasing the street
like it's some lackadaisical gorgeous bubble of soap,
don't you know the torqued cars
have tired Friday men and women in them? Your blue
is the gray of the sky, the gray of the street.
You're one more newsprint face mistaking risk for happiness—I've seen you
coasting prone, chest to skateboard,
wings outstretched low over the fast ground
that falls to the corner, also at dusk and lightened then too
by casting off your outgrown jacket
just as you have your caution. I'm glad you aren't my boy.
Not yet. But this is the street we live on too and do you
occupy his someday space?
And will his cold face come then in the yellow warm? Go home.

Exact Change

Not the seasons,
which steal in,
then sink back for a nap
in the lap of the last.

Nor aging,
which takes years,
and which we may
think to ward off
with surgery or drink.

It's conviction,
coming to us all at once,
be it in the field of
law or politics or love.

Philosophy

Life without language would be
a registration of the sensual:
Sunbeam. Warm. Move onto rock.
Something rather reptilian.
Not bad. Just immediate. Direct.

At times we may believe we crave exactly that.
Let me crawl into a tent.
Bring me the speech of the waves on the sand.

This isn't what we want.
There would be no banter. No excuses.
No clear directions. We'd never get back.

Each crème brûlée would have to be
something come upon
accidentally with eggs—
Sweet. Rich. Move into mouth—
and we'd want another taste of that.

The Kindergartners

All their lives they've waited for
the yellow bus to come for them.
Now it's February and the mat
is wet. The jointed door has folded
back and shut again more times
than any one of them can count.
It has no novelty for them now.
It goes without mention.

The kindergartners ride along,
subdued and quiet. That boy is gone
who hit and kicked and was assigned
all fall as seatmate to our son—
a detail told so late to us,
by then there was nothing to be done.
The mother of the boy had died,
the boy had been sent to stay
in Coppock with his father.

We stand in the mornings in doorways,
blinking back the sun that glints
from either side of the blue caverns
their boots leave behind.
We would do more than wave.
These paths straggle jagged through
our buried yards, registries
of wind and intention.

This Happened Rather Quickly in Slow Motion

I couldn't have been more than three blocks from our house, when I distinctly heard my son call from behind me and across the street. His voice reached me with that extra weight annoyance sometimes gives it now, although usually he tempers this when we're outside the house, yet almost instantly I knew it really wasn't him. Since when would he run outside and three blocks more to catch up with me—and for what?—not even at the long-ago but capable age of nine. I looked to the houses to my right and back for the figure of the teenaged boy who sent out, "Mom," exactly like my son. I turned further and circled sight all the way around. But when all the lawns were seen to be clear of human forms and the homes stood sealed against the season, turned and faced toward winter without any mediating leaves, why did I think to look up then and just in time to glimpse the geese, the one goose, aloof, and closest overhead, and repeating now its sound, not all that much like "Mom"? (One winter will break off, one spring and then a summer, gone.) I suppose to realize that when that corner's turned, the sound and sight of him will be in range only after intervals of time that lengthen unpredictably, and with what joy abruptly stop.

Right This Way, This Way to My Heart

Just tell me the truth, I kept insisting, as if this
would guarantee solidity
where I might blindly turn to put my foot,
could parch the swamps or lay a plank across
the precipice, even though the world is round
and caught up in its own routine: humming
counter-clockwise to itself and all the while engaged
elliptically with other ones around the star.
I know there is no substance to the sounds you make.
(And yet you do make sounds; they might as well
be true, as not.) There it is again,
expectant, embedded, demanding,
and so come one by one the little mutinies.
Also, intermittently, the flashings clear
and brief to beguile and confound me.

Long Dance, Slow Revolution

When two people,
opposites perhaps
in many ways, have lived together
for a long time, she bringing
masterful dinners to the table
with seasonings he would never
have guessed could belong
so well in such sauces,
and he bringing a close to the day
with talk that enriches and plays with all that is common
between them and this continues through the years
of having all their children,
and then one day
he cooks something superb,
although it isn't one of her recipes,
she feels two things.
She feels moved aside
one-half inch
and she feels delight,
as any master does, in what has been learned
and delight, as any lover does,
in the bright change in the beloved.
Things go on as before,
until he does it again,
and more.
A few years pass,
and to everyone's surprise,
at the wedding of her niece,

she stands and is eloquent.
Her words come from a place
standing far back, standing very still,
and what they understand from there
is considerable.
Surely,
at some performance
you have seen two people
dance like this, in syncopation.
It is a long dance, and midway through,
out there in the audience,
you begin to notice
subtle changes,
a borrowing between the parts,
and in the choreography
an increased reciprocity, until
gradually it has become apparent
a reversal has taken place.
You are weeping
and cannot say why.
Something you are surprised to find
you have wanted all along
has been, in gesture, named.

Somewhere Else

When the ground is hard, unresponsive to the step,
unforgiving, or worse, when the slush is as dark
as the street and as heavy as sand, when the sun as a body
has not been seen for several days and only leaks
a little light vaguely, my father knows to call,
the sun a concentrate, potent in his voice.
For a moment I think he's glad to speak to me.
Then he asks me what our weather's like today.
And then I see him where he really is. In retirement.
Near my mother who puts the dishes back on the shelf.
He is sitting on a tall stool at the counter bar
by the kitchen phone and the sliding glass door
that leads to a patio of terra cotta, dry and warm.
They are still in that half of the year they live in Arizona.
Why can't I muster up a little lie for once
and answer with the weather from the week before
—snowpack squeaking underneath my boots,
the streets quieted and waiting, high oak limbs
letting go the one old note of an old door
slowly swinging open? We have so many resources,
so they say, we humans. At the very least, we surely
have more ways to speak than those we've so far
chosen to. I remember waking to the wide blue sky
and the mountains and sun in the one week of warmth
stolen for me every spring. Oh, I surrendered. I can remember
from the age of seven, surrender and resistance, both.
The space invaded my head with an ache,
and the bright weight of the sky thrummed everything outside.

The beauty of the desert was steady and the sun was steady,
and I felt myself aging at remarkable speed.
I crawled out of the pool, my vision glistening.
I blinked and was eight. I lay down in the sun and let
evaporation prick a path through my suit
along the ladder of my ribs and I was ten.
I ate another sugared date and was eleven.
Dad turned left at an old hollow saguaro
on a road in the foothills that eventually just stopped,
and we were lost and I was twelve. "This happens every
time we try to get to this place," my mother said.
I was thirteen when our steaks arrived, toothpicks
stuck into them with curly tops, and fourteen this time
when I plucked out mine. My footprints were behind me,
wet on the cement. I lay down wet and got up dry
and left a shape with hips and breasts. I was sixteen.
But for my parents I guess Arizona might be
something closer to eternity.

III≈

This will remind you of who has abandoned you;

if not, winter
will.

And this will remind you of what you forsook;

if not, spring
will.

And this will remind you of what has found you and welcomed you;

if not, summer
will.

And this will remind you of the good you've withstood;

if not, fall
will.

Cold Cereal and Milk at 3 A.M.

What can make something so simple taste so good,
so indulgent? What have I done, and what have I not,
what have I said, what have I sent that comes back now,
willed or misapplied, in a boomerang of harm?

This is a time of holding in the mouth, of chewing slowly
even these softened squares. The body is comforted by this
as it has been by the remembered scent of those I have loved
who are far and gone from me and dead. Brought close
with their completed lives, they seem to have known me wholly.

Even this wheat-sweetened milk is delicious. And when one
sunken piece turns up—a surprise ending—its gray ghost
stirred and revealed, a small celebration takes place then,
under the ribbed ceiling, near the back of the gums.

Covenant

October, and the chrysanthemums are not without ambition.
To bloom, if only for one week, is then the paramount ambition.

Quickly he judged the levels above him and the relevant adjacencies.
He'd not forget; he'd isolate that shape and name the fault ambition.

Long before the marsh god was born, a place was determined. Where the tide
drenched the shore, where the wind tore the tree, there crouched ambition.

When we are young we reserve a space in the heart for the outside chance.
When we are old, we drowse, then startle: white-out! Inviolate ambition!

In an agreement between yourself and your desires, there is a future self
the self moves toward. Even when the work is good, we can't discount ambition.

We hardly know what to do with the infant we adore. We can feed the child,
but he will choose which to favor: compassion, love, doubt, ambition.

Did you leave the worn corridors behind you, did you venture forth?
Surprised to find yourself here, are you, so plain in your cloth ambition?

A Continual Effort

And if we stopped our improving and left everything as is?
Unhelped, the desert could return to its scarcity basis.

Landslide of papers, slivers of straw and glass, a toppled lamp.
Don't disturb the evidence. Leave everything as is.

When God looked at all that had been done he said, "I'm spent.
My imagination's drained. This is how it finishes."

In the clamor of choices, nothing had seemed good and sufficient.
He'd slumped and sighed and said, "Leave everything as is."

When you send back silence, or answer, instead, a question
unasked, it's your quiet or question then that is.

What if we stopped taking photographs at Christmas?
Would we really not remember if we hadn't any images?

Here I go again, knee-deep through the leaves, knowing
full well now, and with what regularity, everything changes.

Tumbleweed

In the end, one naturally asks the question, "Who is speaking, and why?"
The impulse to eavesdrop begins with it: *who is speaking, and why.*

The teacher stopped mid-sentence and dropped his hands to the lectern.
The silence spread back before he'd asked them who was speaking and why.

The sun sets and rises. Weeds tremble in the fencing. A train goes by.
We'll never learn the nameless location, who is speaking, and why.

The effigies were drenched, punctured, smeared, but they settled the score.
At such an event no one need mention who is speaking and why.

Is it the judge this time, the sergeant, the statesman, or the entrepreneur?
What is meant here by "requisition?" Who is speaking and why?

Omission isn't mystery to me. Detachment isn't of interest.
I'd like to know a bit of the rest, and who is speaking, and why.

MMI–MMVII

I come to you from a broad silence.
I have tried to speak from the old continuity, but the awkwardness remains.
Is it that I cannot see you, is that why?

When Sondra Duarte died, deer appeared by the roadside.
One and then two more great bucks came forward on the lawns.
Other deaths were still near to me then. My mother's,
with its tubes and fluids and gases,
with its enormous restrictions. A rigid death.
My father's, only two months behind, his death and the death
of his terror. And of course others followed
on the other side. In July of one year, and in March and in June of the next.
In August my mother-in-law looked up
into the face of her eldest son
and said, just one day beforehand, *It's my turn now,*
and she was not a religious woman, but it felt then to me
as if she'd been more or less waiting,
peering out from behind her sisters
and her half sisters, her parents.
And as each of these one by one left their lives, I watched
others I loved let failure into theirs as if they were simply
watching from the side,
and Bush's war droned on. "Droned on," that's how it's said.
A noise weaving in and out of our consciousness, stepping up,
stepping back. *Oh yes,* we remember. *That.*

I can imagine that yours is a silence not unlike my own.
It may be that mine has been a silence not entirely my own.

And so I can step to you out of the vegetable garden
at its turn towards autumn,
the yellow crook neck squash sprawled across the paths and onto
neighboring beds in all its unmanageable vigor,
the pole beans producing despite the bug-ridden laciness of their leaves.
I step over the speechless stink of a cabbage,
over a few tomatoes already fallen. I step over thyme and savory,
roots still curled tight and green, their outer edges creeping,
the plant spreading. I step down backwards from the attic
where herbs hang upside down from the rafters, labels dangling,
oregano, mint, lemongrass, thyme,
and garlic hangs braided in bunches alongside the shallots and onions
and the least breeze disturbs their loosening skins, and they fall,
and the next one stirs them with a little dust.
And I come to the sink where I wash
what I have carried from the garden. And if you followed,
if you were here, listening, you could hear the water
sliding over the bright skins of peppers.
I turn the water on and off, but this isn't speech, it isn't thinking.
You could hear the disturbance when each leaf of lettuce
is lifted from the water, shaken twice in the air
and dropped gently into the glinting sieve.
Then you could hear the crickets instead.

Prayer

1.

To slowly make out the shape
of all of this, which is to think.
(To be able to package it, a small weight in the hand,
to be able to throw it against the wall,
to hear the sound it would make.)

(A dull sound from a solid object.)

To think with an imagined audience of one.

2.

A friend of my mother's used to pray for parking spaces.

3.

A person could tell a lot about us
by the way that we pray.

When someone prays, *Help me with this problem,*
it might mean *Solve it.*
Or, *show me the way.*

A person could tell a lot about God
by the way that we pray.

4.

Can our gestures be seen?
Are the hands quieted or are they utilized?
Is there reason to raise the face heavenward?

5.
Is much context provided, or is this
presumed known?

6.
Does the Presence stay with us for the long
weeping part, or are we thought
to be put on hold?

7.
Sometimes we resign ourselves
to another mortal instead—a stranger
seated next to us, a cat, a dog, a friend—

and what is said has a quality
common in fiction, less so in life.

Short, abrupt sentences trip up,
entangled in the longer ones
that are being thought. Only frayed
and intermittent connections
tie cause to result.

When a listener hears through the confusion
to the pit-shape of need,
what then is to be done with this love?

Praemeditatio

after Seneca

Touch the rudder lightly, Fortune,
and bring me to some shore I know I don't deserve.
My actions have been purposeful sometimes
and still have come to naught,
caused harm or self-deception.
I don't know what the water is, but that I float or swim
or, helped by something that wants to help
or helps despite its wants, am kept for now
from one more ending no more random
than my life. *Give us a push, then*
(as the old soul, smiling to us, said)
since chance divisions and unknown
fortitudes have brought me into being
and in order to express my gratitude
I must select my suspects from a list
I haven't seen. Someone has been buried
everywhere my foot has stepped and every place
the shadow of my other foot has crossed.

The Anxiety of the Pilgrim

The pheasant flew up on our left
from the endless corn.

The clouds were low, dark, dramatic,
full of movement, but I knew it wouldn't rain.

I wanted the car to go on by itself
so that I could watch the color of the clouds
fix the color of the corn.

Even if we catch no fish, I thought,
even if it rains,

I've seen a place pulled up
in the form of a bird. I've seen the form
of a bird falling into place.

We had to be nearing the end of things
happening in ways we hadn't asked for
and didn't welcome as surprise.

And it didn't really rain.
A little mist in early morning.

The brown trout were not so lucky now.

And when we walked for water, later,
eight hollow knocks shuddered out
from the trunk of an oak.

It's not a power of mine: the confidence
that things will turn out right in the end.

That's why any change at all is presumed to have weight.
That's why any sound is the sound of arrival.

Every streak of luck will break.

We may think that we haven't the courage

but all is to be dared, because even a person of poverty
can feel the ice, with its new coat of water,
slip beneath her shoes.

There are more ways than eyes,
and there is a breaking up to every solid matter.

The forces who determine that long wars will carry over
into the next column,
the brother who despises me for my plain nature,
even these can be shocked into new logics.
It might be the look of a snake that does it,
or the entrails of a fox.

There are plates that shift and quake
and alter other matters slightly or greatly.

If I didn't believe this, I wouldn't turn over and get up.
If I didn't believe this I wouldn't plant a thing.
I wouldn't read another poem.

To encapsulate the unattainable, you speak to me of work

but I to you of a white goat.
I say how the goat escapes, always, just as a piece of it
has become visible to me. Above the bark of a fallen tree,
I saw the topmost ridge of hair along the back of the white goat,
gone as I focused harder. To the side of the cabin
a little ways off, I glimpsed the paintbrush tail of the white goat.
I imagined the neck bent to the hostas,
a luscious stand of them below the small rear window.
And what peered at me in traffic through two slots
in a livestock truck but the face of the white goat? I stared, incredulous,
as it passed me to merge with traffic headed towards Toledo.

These are the subjects we endure
in order that we may better understand each other.
And consider how different they are: the coyness and carelessness
and striving of your co-workers, the appearances of the goat;
the routine revamping of technologies you depend on,
and the intangibility of the goat. This evening I reported:
"Today, the first spring-like day! How the goat
would have enjoyed it!" All morning, as I worked in the yard
removing old leaves and old growth, I pictured him
standing on the grassy mound (not much longer or wider than himself),
to get a better view of the neighbors' crocus.

Notes

"Allocation" is informed by cases and questions raised by bioethicist, author, and advisor on genetic and reproductive technology Lori Andrews in *The Clone Age: Adventures in the New World of Reproductive Technology* (Henry Holt and Company, 1999). See especially p. 4, pp. 213–214.

The first lines in four poems are fragments from Sappho, as follows:

"Untitled" (*whiter by far than an egg*)

"This will remind you of who has abandoned you;" (*if not, winter*)

"We may think that we haven't the courage" (*but all is to be dared, because even a person of poverty*)

"To encapsulate the unattainable, you speak to me of work" (*but I to you of a white goat*)

The translations are Anne Carson's from *If Not, Winter; Fragments of Sappho* (Knopf, 2002). They are from fragments 167, 22, 31, and 40, respectively.

"MMI–MMVII": I believe that I first heard the phrase, "Bush's War," in the poem so titled by Robert Hass in *Time and Materials: Poems 1997–2005* (Harper Collins, 2007).

"To encapsulate the unattainable, you speak to me of work" owes an unintentional debt to the specially designated chicken in the poem by Jane Mead, "Passing a Truck Full of Chickens at Night on Highway Eighty," in *The Lord and the General Din of the World* (Sarabande, 1986). I may never be able to remove that yearning chicken from the reserve of influential images in my mind.

Iowa Poetry Prize and
Edwin Ford Piper Poetry Award Winners

1987   Elton Glaser, *Tropical Depressions*
       Michael Pettit, *Cardinal Points*

1988   Bill Knott, *Outremer*
       Mary Ruefle, *The Adamant*

1989   Conrad Hilberry, *Sorting the Smoke*
       Terese Svoboda, *Laughing Africa*

1990   Philip Dacey, *Night Shift at the Crucifix Factory*
       Lynda Hull, *Star Ledger*

1991   Greg Pape, *Sunflower Facing the Sun*
       Walter Pavlich, *Running near the End of the World*

1992   Lola Haskins, *Hunger*
       Katherine Soniat, *A Shared Life*

1993   Tom Andrews, *The Hemophiliac's Motorcycle*
       Michael Heffernan, *Love's Answer*
       John Wood, *In Primary Light*

1994   James McKean, *Tree of Heaven*
       Bin Ramke, *Massacre of the Innocents*
       Ed Roberson, *Voices Cast Out to Talk Us In*

2005 Emily Rosko, *Raw Goods Inventory*
Joshua Marie Wilkinson, *Lug Your Careless Body out of the Careful Dusk*

2006 Elizabeth Hughey, *Sunday Houses the Sunday House*
Sarah Vap, *American Spikenard*

2008 Andrew Michael Roberts, *something has to happen next*
Zach Savich, *Full Catastrophe Living*

2009 Samuel Amadon, *Like a Sea*
Molly Brodak, *A Little Middle of the Night*

2010 Julie Hanson, *Unbeknownst*
L. S. Klatt, *Cloud of Ink*